PRELIMINARY REMARKS ON THE ROYAL PALACE OF EBLA

by

Paolo Matthiae
University of Rome

This article presents a preliminary picture of the 1973-1[illegible] excavations of the Tell Mardikh Royal Palace G dating to Early Bronze IVA (ca. 2400-2250 B.C.). It was in 1975 that some 15,000 cuneiform tablets and fragments were found in the palace, some of them written in a new North-Western Semitic language. The various sectors of the palace thus far excavated are described and the building is placed within its chronological and historical framework. Ceramic evidence pertaining to the chronology is published here in detail for the first time. The paper (given here in a translation by Dr. Frances Pinnock) was read at the 24th Rencontre Assyriologique Internationale at Birmingham in July 1976.

Table of Contents

Introduction: Ceramic and Epigraphic Evidence for Chronology

The thick mud brick structures identified at Tell Mardikh (Fig. 1) by the Italian Archaeological Mission to Syria in 1973 were dated by us to Early Bronze IV (ca. 2400-2000 B.C.), presumably in an initial stage of its development. This could be done despite the small number of sherds collected on what turned out to be the southern ramp of the so-called "Ceremonial Staircase" (L.2525). These structures were located in sector G on the western slope of the Acropolis, in the area of Square DIV6. The enlargement, in 1974, of the excavations to the North and to the West of the tower which contained the staircase made us exclude the hypothesis that the tower belonged to a defensive system of the Acropolis erected in the last centuries of the IIIrd millennium B.C. Our investigations in 1974 led, on the contrary, to a correlation of the imposing remains of mud brick walls with Building G, probably a Palace, the extension of which still appeared quite uncertain (Matthiae 1975, 350-51, Figs. 4-5). The extension of the excavations in 1975 to the East, South and West of the already exposed area of Building G made it possible to fix the limits of the monument to the West and, through a notable enlargement of the digging to the South and some soundings to the East, to identify the nature and functions of the structures (Fig. 2). Though the monument as so far excavated is surely quite limited in comparison with its original extent, it is evident that Building G was one of the royal administrative buildings of the Acropolis of Ebla (Matthiae and Pettinato 1976, 25-28). It was probably built around 2400 B.C. and destroyed about 2250 B.C. (Matthiae 1976a, 199-203). These chronological indications essentially derive from the evidence that the Royal Palace G of Ebla belonged to the archaeological horizon of Mardikh IIB1, (see Table, p. 9) which corresponds to Early Bronze IVA (ca. 2400-2250 B.C.) of Northern Syria, a phase contemporary with the so-called Protoimperial Period and with part of the dynasty of Akkad in Mesopotamia (M. J. Mellink, in Ehrich, R. W. [ed.] 1965, 101-27).

The ceramic evidence (Fig. 3-4) of Mardikh IIB1 is very close to Amuq I, with the only important exception of the "Red-Black Burnished Ware," completely absent in Mardikh IIB1 levels and attributed to Amuq I (Braidwood and Braidwood 1960, 398-403; but see Tadmor 1964, especially pp. 261-63). The level of Palace G of Mardikh IIB1 is characterized by a clear predominance of "Simple Ware": the goblets with flat bases and corrugated surfaces and the bowls with thickened and rounded rims are frequent. Much less frequent, but typical, are the egg-shaped jars and the small spouted jars of corrugated ware with centrally flat ring base. In the "Painted Simple Ware" category, while the painted goblets of Hama J (Fugmann 1958, 64-80) are completely absent, one finds small jars with bands of red or black paint and typical juglets with black paint in bands or plaits. Sherds of "Reserved Slip Ware" are documented in only small percentages. "Smeared Wash Ware," which is typical of Early Bronze IVB and of Amuq J (Braidwood and Braidwood 1960, 446-50), is completely absent here.

This evaluation of the archaeological evidence for the chronology of the Royal Palace G had found, in the first readings of the texts of the State Archives of the archive L.2769 by G. Pettinato, what appeared like a definitive confirmation since some Ebla documents reportedly contained the name of the city of Akkad (Pettinato 1976b, 12). This identification seemed to give a positive proof to the hypothesis, formulated even before the finding of the State Archives in September-October 1975, that the destruction of Palace G at Ebla was due to Naram-Sin of Akkad (Matthiae 1975, 355-56). The hypothesis of the destruction of Palace G by Naram-Sin was, moreover, confirmed by the plausible identification with Sargon of Akkad of one Shariginu, mentioned in one of the largest commercial accounts (TM.75.G.2428) of the Ebla Archives. This name on the tablet was located at a very short distance from the title EN A.EN.GA.DU^{ki}, that is, according to the reading just cited, "king of Akkad" (Matthiae 1976a, 210). Since this document is dated to the time of Ibrium of Ebla and since it is known from the bulk of the evidence provided by the texts of the State Archives that the destruction of Palace G happened during the second generation after Ibrium, in the time of Dubukhu-Ada, Ibrium's grandson, it appeared evident that there was a chronological correspondence between the destruction and Naram-Sin, Sargon's grandson.

Now, after a restudy of the pertinent texts, the mention of the city of Akkad in the Ebla texts appears possible but not certain. The absolute chronology of the Royal Palace G and of the dynasty of the kings of Ebla who appear in the texts of the State Archives has then essentially two possibilities: either the Royal Palace of Ebla has been destroyed by Sargon of Akkad around 2300 B.C. (Gadd 1966, 11-12) and the dynasty of Ebla with its first king Igrish-Khalam began its reign around 2450 B.C., or the destruction was due to Naram-Sin of Akkad around 2250 B.C. and the dynasty started around 2400 B.C. (Matthiae 1976b, 15, 16). The paleographic evidence for the archaizing character of the documents of the State Archives (Pettinato 1976a, 51-52; Gelb 1977) is more favorable to the first of these hypothesis, while the complex of archaeological evidence seems to favor the second (Matthiae 1976a, 198-203). The historical data too would make us prefer the second hypothesis. In copies of Sargon's inscriptions it is said that the god Dagan of Tuttul gave to the great king of Akkad Armanum, Yarmuti, Mari and Ebla (Kupper and Sollberger 1971, IIA1b). However, Naram-Sin is much more explicit; he boasts in fact of the conquest of Armanum and Ebla, a city never conquered, according to his own words, since the creation of mankind till his own days (Hirsch 1963, 73-75; Kupper and Sollberger 1971, IIA4b,e,q).

Description of Sectors Excavated

The part of the Royal Palace G so far excavated lies on the south-western slope of the Acropolis (Pl. 1). It was built on terraces on the slopes of the ancient tell made by the ruins of constructions of Early Bronze III (ca. 2750-2400 B.C.) and of earlier periods; these are documented not only by some very limited architectural remains, but also by a statuette fragment (Matthiae 1974, 125-37) and by scattered pieces of figurative limestone inlays (Dolce 1975, 289-306). The excavations have brought to light thus far the following sectors of Palace G: a large part of an "Audience Court" with its porch; some small rooms behind the North façade of the Court used as storerooms; two rooms situated further North; a massive tower with a "Ceremonial Staircase" of four ramps situated in the intersection between the North and East façades of the Court; and very small parts of two other rooms behind the East façade of the same Court.

What remains of the North façade of the large "Audience Court" has been excavated to the extent of 16 m. (Figs. 2 and 6). To the West, toward the Lower City, it is interrupted by both erosion and the reconstructions of Early Bronze IVB (ca. 2250-2000 B.C.) and of Middle Bronze I (ca. 2000-1800 B.C.); these have reduced the level of the Palace. In fact, on the same axis as the door which opened immediately to the West of the royal podium on the thick wall M.2614, on the northern façade of the Court, a wall in bricks of the same size as the big bricks of the Palace of Mardikh IIB1 was built. This happened soon after the destruction of the Royal Palace G, i.e. during Early Bronze IVB, corresponding to Mardikh IIB2. The function of this structure, preserved only for a short stretch one brick course high, cannot be determined, but it may have been due to a desire to limit to the West the region of the ruins of the Royal Palace G. The East façade of the "Audience Court" has been exposed for a long stretch of about 25 m., but surely it continues in a good state of preservation toward the South beyond the actual limit of the excavations.

Under the porch of the North façade there rose a plastered rectangular podium of clay bricks, 4.5 m. wide and 3 m. long, upon which the royal throne must have been placed (Pl. 4). On the North façade to the West of the podium a door opened which put the Court in communication with the narrow storerooms behind the North façade and also possibly with the two large rooms built further North, L.2586 and L.2601. The difference of level between the storeroom L.2617 built behind the North façade of the Court and the room L.2586 is about 3.80 m. Since the slope of the Acropolis has obliterated completely the West sectors of L.2586 and L.2601 and since, therefore, there are no data to establish the placement of the terracing wall which supported the two rooms, it is impossible to say if there was a connection–and, if so, to establish the nature of this connection to the West of the storeroom L.2617 and L.2586.

At the East end of the northern porch was the high and narrow entrance to the "Ceremonial Staircase," built inside the tower and richly decorated on all the steps with inlays, set into wooden planks, of different floral-geometric decorations (Pls. 2, 3, 5-8). The richness and delicacy of this decoration of the steps of the four ramps make it probable that the "Ceremonial Staircase" was used only by the king and his dignitaries in occasion of audiences. It is therefore likely that it connected the royal apartments, presumed to have been on an upper storey in the building complex limited by the East façade, with the podium of the royal throne in the "Audience Court." It is important to point out that the "Ceremonial Staircase" must have ended on the West side with a fourth ramp, either partially aereal or perhaps going on with a fifth completely aereal ramp on the South side; though the high structures have not preserved any trace of it, the upper door leading to the superior apartments had to open respectively, according to the two different hypothesis, either on the South or on the East side. It does not seem likely on the contrary that the Staircase might have led to a true second floor of the building, but rather to the ground floor, much higher, to the East of the front of M.2565: however only further investigations to the East of M.2565, will make clear the types of communications used inside the Royal Palace G and in its Northern annexes. For the moment one can only point out that between the only two limited sectors excavated to the East of M.2751, the East façade of the Court, that is between L.2834 to the North and L.2764 to the South there is a difference in elevation of 1.20 m.

On the East façade, in a position asymmetrical to this façade, a portal opened; it was preceded by three steps made from limestone slabs, while the threshold on which the wooden doors must have swung was bordered by two long basalt monoliths (Pl. 9). Below the East porch a room, L.2769, about 3.5 m. wide had been made with partitions only one brick thick; its roof was probably much lower than the roof of the porch. This room, the length of which was certainly more than 4 m., though it cannot be determined with precision since the excavations have not reached the South wall, was the Court archive or, more probably, one of the rooms below the East porch used for the archives (Matthiae 1976d, 30-34). In fact, taking into consideration the square DiV4ii and in particular the South-western corner of this square, where, though the floor of the Court is well preserved, there is no trace of the South structure of the Court, one must think that the archive L.2769 continued to the South of the square DiV4ii [see now Matthiae 1977, 247]. Moreover in the South wall of this same square the presence of a pilaster has been verified; it was built with the long side oriented East-West, instead of North-South like the one in the North-East corner of L.2769. Therefore, this pilaster must have been built to facilitate the placing of the East shelving, similar to the other pilaster of the room which helped to support the North shelving. If, therefore, the South pilaster was put at an angle like the North-Western one, it is clear that the South wall of L.2769 was a partition wall like the North wall M.2768. This South wall does not continue to the West beyond the porch since it is not attested in the South-West area of the square DiV4ii, as I have already mentioned. Consequently, it appears that there are only two possible hypotheses in a reconstruction of this area: either L.2769 was a small room limited by three partition walls to the North, West and South, and was therefore isolated below the East proch, or it was the North end of two or more rooms built at the extreme South of the East porch, like L.2712 (Pls. 12 and 13).

In this room, L.2769, nearly 14,000 cuneiform tablets and fragments of tablets of the State Archives were found. These tablets, which are mainly accounts of international textile trade controlled by the central authority, were kept on three wooden shelves of regular depth, ca. 0.80 m., and height, ca. 0.50 m., set against the walls and sustained by rectangular wooden supports (Fig. 5 and Pls. 14 and 15) (Matthiae 1976, 255-61).

At the North end of the East porch a smaller room, L.2712, about 2.5 by 2.7 m. wide, was used to preserve tablets dealing in large part with the delivery of food and drinks for the journeys of messengers and ambassadors (Pl. 12). The tablets and fragments, one thousand in inventory numbers, were originally arranged on two shelves, probably wooden. These have been lost but traces of them have remained in the plaster of the North and East walls, M.2550 and M.2751. The only entrance to the storeroom L.2712 opened in the South partition wall and led to the "Audience Court." This same entry position can probably be reconstructed for the library L.2769, the entrance of which has not yet been found [see now Matthiae 1977, 247].

Behind the East façade two soundings carried out in squares EaV6iii and DIV4i brought to light very small sections of two rooms. The one to the North, L.2834, must have been used as a storeroom since against one of the walls, M.2833, a large bench of unbaked bricks had been built. In this bench were walled large jars for the storage of wheat. To the South the other room, L.2764, could have been an archive as two benches of different heights and one brick thick had been built against the East façade, M.2751; some 30 fragments of cuneiform tablets were scattered on the floor (Pl. 10). The function of the benches of L.2764 is not yet clear. In seeking an answer to this problem one must take into consideration the objects found in the room, among which there are several necklace beads with the characteristic rounded morphology slightly flattened at the poles, typical of Mardikh IIB1, and a noteworthy fragment of inlay with the figure of a sheep. This Palace room is however without a direct connection to the Court, unlike the storeroom L.2712 and the library L.2769.

The "Audience Court" (Fig. 6), of which two sides, the North and East, have been excavated, was more than 31 m. long on the North-South axis and more than 25 m. East to West. These two measurements are the real sizes of the Court and not of the East and North façades only; these façades are shorter due to the space occupied in comparison with the area of the Court, by the tower of the "Ceremonial Staircase" (Pls. 2, 3). The preserved North and East façades so far excavated were not exactly perpendicular but slightly converging, while the tower of the "Ceremonial Staircase" forms a unitary block perfectly homogeneous with the North façade. Though the walls surrounding the Court are consistenly 2.8 m. thick and the bricks everywhere of the same type measuring 0.60 by 0.40 m., it seems probable that only the tower and the North façade were planned at the same time, while later on the East façade was added against the North complex. In fact, the building of the Court structures must have caused some surprises of a static order, not foreseen in the planning phase by its builders, as may be inferred from the presence of the two big buttresses of the tower containing the staircase. Also the intercolumnations of the East porch, varying between 3.2 and 3.4 m., differ from those of the North porch which constantly measure 4.1 m.; the column sockets, regular round holes 0.80 m. deep, are everywhere the same, 0.70 m. There are no sure indications of the height of the columns, but the structures preserved show no trace of the insertions of beams belonging to the coverings of the porch. One must therefore conclude that the columnades of the Court must have been more than 5.3 m. high, this being the greatest height of the structures preserved in the North-East area of the complex.

Functional Analysis of Excavated Areas

If one now tries to sum up the descriptive data so far illustrated in order to formulate some interpretations of the functions of each sector of the Royal Palace G brought to light up to now, it seems possible on one hand to point out some sure data and on the other to formulate some likely hypothesis. Among the former one must underline the public function of the "Audience Court" in the sense one can give to the term in the Near East during 24th century B.C. That it was a Court for public audiences appears from the presence of the royal podium, from the closeness of the "Ceremonial Staircase" and from the decoration of big stone eyes which probably ran on a thin, continuous frieze at the height of 1.85 m. along the two walls of the porch [see Matthiae 1977, 249]. None of the stone eyes found in the Court has been found *in situ*, but this may result from the fact that they were probably set into a wooden fillet or on the edge of a narrow wooden shelf. This fillet, or shelf, was in turn set into the wall of the Court in the location where one can now clearly see a rectlinear crack on the surface of the plaster. This crack extends entirely across both the North and East façades.

The business transacted in the "Audience Court" can be deducted from the contents of the documents preserved in the library L.2769, and in the smaller storeroom, L.2712, both rooms which, it must be stressed, one could enter only from the Court. These are, for the greatest part, accounts of deliveries of textiles to dignitaries of the city and to representatives of foreign cities for their sovereigns; lists of tributes and taxes mostly in silver and gold received through high dignitaries of the state; receipts of deliveries of food rations for missions of ambassadors and messengers to cities often very far away. It should also be kept in mind that among the documents less well represented are a very few abstracts of international treaties which are evidently copies for the use of the royal chancery of Ebla, in addition to lexical and literary texts which show the existence of schools clearly connected with the central administration; royal edicts regarding several juridical and administrative problems, such as the concession of some cities of the kingdom to princes of the royal family; letters reporting to the king of Ebla successful military campaigns like the one concerning the victory of Enna-Dagan, a high dignitary of Ebla, against Iblul-Il, king of Mari and Assur (Matthiae 1976a, 210-11).

From this quite short and partial picture of the subjects treated in the documents of Ebla royal archives from rooms L.2712 and L.2769, it clearly appears that the "Audience Court" had, at least prevalently if not exclusively, a specific function. In it one dealt with foreign trade above all and in the second place with the exaction of tributes. More particularly, it could be imagined that in the Court the business connected with the distribution of the textiles produced under state control was attended to as well as the material payment of the taxes owed the state by functionaries, governors and vassals. Concerning the dispatch of this type of business, the royal officials wanted to provide a large open space available in the "Audience Court" as opposed to the closed space of a throne room. In this connection it is likely that the Court was, at least partially, the initial staging area for caravans charged with the shipment of textiles, hence the need for a wide open space. In this interpretation, the frieze with eyes which, with its obsessive repetition of the sight organ, could symbolize the inexorable and infallible acuteness of the royal and divine justice, would plausibly assume a particularly pregnant meaning. This function of the Court is further proven by the discovery in the storeroom L.2712 of a group of basalt and limestone weights which were perhaps preserved there to measure the amounts of metal deliveries to the Palace.

When, as it seems very likely, one attributes to the "Audience Court" a specific rather than a generic function connected with determined activities of government and in particular with the handling of affairs pertaining to foreign relations and state finances, one obtains a functional explanation for the storerooms behind the North façade. Of the rooms built behind the North façade of the Court, L.2617 was a narrow corridor which contained jars mostly for liquids, while the small room L.2716 had a few jars in the corners and many remains of bullae with cylinder seal impressions which must have sealed not only pots, (one of which, at least, was of metal) but also caskets. One could assume the same for the two rooms located further North, which may have been used for administrative and public relations purpose: this is documented by the discovery on the floor of one of the rooms of about 40 cuneiform tablets of an economic character, and, in another room of considerable remains of very valuable wood inlays belonging to a piece of furniture of great artistic value (Matthiae 1975, 351-55) (Pls. 16 and 17).

Although the exploration of the area East of the "Audience Court" is still in too preliminary a phase to permit sound overall judgements it can be noted that the "Ceremonial Staircase" in the tower indicates a royal passage and confirms the supposition that upper storeys existed for the royal apartments. This supposition would explain the great thickness of the walls at least of the East structures, while rooms used for archives or offices opened to the ground floor and had thinner walls. In the palatial architecture of the Syrian area of the Old Syrian period, the hypothesis of upper floors has been reasonably proposed for the palace of Alalakh VII (Woolley 1955, 93-95), while the huge perimetrical structure of Naram-Sin's palace at Tell Brak could make us think of fortifications on an upper floor (Mallowan 1947, 63-66). Even though after the destruction of the Royal Palace G of Ebla, probably by Naram-Sin of Akkad, the area East of the "Ceremonial Staircase" was covered by a wide monumental stone stairway (Pl. 11) built during Early Bronze IVB (ca. 2250-2000 B.C.)–perhaps at the time of the dynasty of Lagash II–thus making the systematic exploration of this part of the Palace difficult, different clues lead us to suppose that smaller rooms to the East and North-East of the tower were used for services.

Spatial Analysis of the "Audience Court" in a Historical Perspective

When from the functional aspects one passes to a consideration of the strictly spatial features of the architecture of the Royal Palace G of Ebla, even with the limitations of the remains discovered till now, the building stands out for the originality of its conception and realization, so that it constitutes an emblematic monument of an architectural civilization which expresses a clear autonomy of language. The Royal Palace G or, to be more precise, the "Audience Court" connected with the Palace is the first monument which shows, in this most significant historical centre of the Early Syrian culture and in an unequivocal archaeological context, the characteristics of the architectural contribution to the civilization of Syria in the IIIrd millennium B.C. We did not have up to now other evidence of this architecture except for some temples of Byblos of uncertain date and some likely western influences present in the archaic temples of Mari (Moortgat 1968, 221-31).

The topographic location of the "Audience Court" on the western slope of the Acropolis, in a somewhat peripheral position in comparison with the presumed residential and administrative quarters of the city, warrants the hypothesis that this large porched space stood not inside but rather outside the Palace complex. The position of the Court in the urban reality of Early Syrian Ebla, and the meaning which must be attributed to it, will be the matter of a future study by the writer. It is certain, however, that one must look for documentary elements which will allow us to understand how the Court was really inserted in the urban pattern of the city; to this aim, as the erosion of the tell and the reconstructions of the Early Syrian period have carried away every bit of evidence for the West sector of the Court, in next campaigns the greatest attention will be paid to the South sector of the Court. This South sector should preserve sound evidence of the type of enclosure of the open space on the sides where with every possibility the palatial buildings did not continue. On the basis of the remains brought to light till now, one would thus be dealing with an *open space* located among non-homogeneous elements of the urban layout, and not with a *closed space* surrounded by similar parts of the same building, as it is not an area typologically defined in function of an organic and unitary palatial structure that encloses it (Margueron 1974, 12-26), but rather a functionally specified area set among differing building entities. In other words that space has an urban rather than an architectural value. The concept which is at the root of this original formulation of the "Audience Court" coordinates distinct but typologically connected structures in planimetric association apparently lacking an organic unity, according to a planning method that from this period on appear to be a constant of the architectural culture of pre-hellenistic Syria (Matthiae in Orthmann 1975, 467, 473, 475-77).

There is, therefore, a substantial difference between the "Audience Court" of late Early Syrian Ebla and the courts of the older palaces of Early Dynastic Mesopotamia. So in Palace "A" of Kish, datable to an initial phase of the Mesilim Period, perhaps around or shortly after 2700 B.C., the court, lost for the greatest part, at the entrance of the North complex, as well as the internal court of the same complex, have a clear distributive function, and on it is based the spatial organization of the single wings (Heinrich in Orthmann 1975, 148, Fig. 14). No different was the value of the Palace "P," the so-called "Plano-Convex Building" of Kish, generally thought to be contemporary to the other Palace, but probably later and datable to the Fara Period, though the planning of this important Early Dynastic building, recently reconstructed according to unpublished notes, shows evident mistakes mostly in the reconstruction of the East corner (Moorey 1964, 85-92, Pl. XXI). The problem of the origin of the palatial typology in Early Dynastic Mesopotamia has to be studied and one can only say that surely it finds an autonomy of formulation not before the end of the First Transition Period or at the beginning of the Mesilim Period, that is between 2800 and 2700 B.C. (Moortgat 1967, 27-28). But it is clear that just this phase of the architectural history of Mesopotamia is characterized by an elaboration and reinterpretation of the spatial value of the old schemes of the Protohistorical Period. Initially this took place through the juxtaposition of a court to the organic temple structure of the Uruk and Jamdat Nasr Periods (Moortgat 1967, 9-15): thus, for example, in the well known series of rebuildings of the Sin

Temple of Khafaje (Delougaz and Lloyd 1942, 5-44). Progressively, however, but certainly already in the Mesilim Period the court assumes a dynamic function in the project. It is no more an equivocal forepart, juxtaposed but really separated from the protohistorical core of the building, but it becomes the productive and organizing fulcrum of the spaces in a new organic vision. From this vision, connected to a conception and to the radically changed reality of the Early Dynastic social structures in comparison to the Protohistorical Period (Moortgat 1967, 29-32), which is clearly reflected in architectural works, come the most characteristic typologies of the Mesilim Period, from the classical *Hofhaustempel* to the oval temple (Heinrich in Orthmann 1975, 133-34). Now, on the one hand, the Early Dynastic Palaces are not, in my opinion, the autonomous planimetric developments of some sectors, maybe administrative ones, of the more complex sacred buildings of the Mesilim Period (Moorey 1964, 93-94). There is no doubt, on the other hand, that the foundations of the palaces of Kish, like those of Mari and Eridu, are, on the basis of a distinct and parallel social and institutional need, an independent result of the same Early Dynastic architectural conception which bases the overall spatial organization around the Court (Heinrich in Orthmann 1975, 146-49). Such a central role of the court is only one of the characteristic planning devices which can be traced along a unitarian line of development from the Mesilim Period down to the fortress-store house of Tell Brak, built by Naram-Sin of Akkad, and to the classical Old Babylonian example of the great palace of Mari [see Y. Al Khalesi, *The Court of the Palms: A Functional Analysis of the Mari Palace,* BM 8, Malibu 1978–Editor's note]. Next to this, other equally characteristic planning devices are asserted, such as the definition of the single parts by means of long perimetrical corridors, clearly evident in the sacred quarter of the Presargonic Palace PP2 of Mari (Parrot 1972, 292-98, Fig. 2); this principle is still working in the large buildings of the sacred enclosure at Ur in the Ur III period (Woolley 1974, 43-44, Pl. 57).

The wide porched Court of Early Syrian Ebla of Early Bronze IVA, founded perhaps around 2400 B.C. under the reign of Igrish-Khalam, the first king for whom documents have been found in the Archives (Matthiae 1976a, 209), appears, on the contrary, completely alien to this development, which in Mesopotamia traces a coherent process in the search for some fundamental spatial conceptions. The "Audience Court" of Ebla is a monument far from the taste of Early Dynastic Mesopotamia: the wide expanse of the horizontal dimensions which could plausibly be even twice the length of those brought to light up to now (this is possible if the podium occupied a central position on the North façade), the scenographic effect of the columnades framing the podium and the Portal given by the shadows reflected from the buttresses of the tower, the lack of spatial relation between the porched façades and the rooms behind them, are all elements which, though in the still very partial state of the excavations, reveal a peculiar Early Syrian elaboration of the palace theme during the 3rd millennium B.C. completely independent from the process of formation of the Mesopotamian palace.

In conclusion, we may formulate two questions for further enquiry. First, could the Syrian vision depend, if not from a *contemporary* Mesopotamian inspiration, (which we have just excluded) then from an *older* Mesopotamian one? In the second place, could this vision be found again in the later tradition of Syria, which depends on it and which it has contributed to build? To the first question, there is a suggestive, albeit hypothetical, answer. If there is a remote Mesopotamian inspiration, this has to be seen in the peculiar organization of the outer spaces of Uruk in the middle phase of the Protohistorical Period, around 3300-3100 B.C. (cf. now Lenzen 1968, 13-18). Were this the case it would lead us to find an important connection between Uruk and Ebla, not strange if one thinks of the clear, and recently verified, typological and chronological relations between Uruk and some protohistorical centres of the upper valley of the Euphrates (Strommenger, in Bahnassi 1974, 55-56), the title EN of the king of Ebla, equivalent to Eblaite *malikum*, would not be accidental, but would confirm very old institutional and cultural common traditions (Matthiae 1976c, 253-66). As for the second question the answer is more certain, and no less significant for the history of culture. Already some years ago our attention was correctly called to the central problem of the continuity of the architectural conception of Syria from the so-called Yarim-Lim's palace of Alalakh VII to the Aramaean citadels of the first millennium

B.C. (Frankfort 1954, 139-40, 167-75). The attention paid to the outer spaces, the fragmentation of the palatial entities, the taste for scenographies all are elements which, though in the apparently broken and dispersed flux of the civilization of Syria, are constant reference points, differently felt and interpreted, in later palaces, from Ugarit, around 1400 B.C. to Samᵓal, between 1000 and 740 B.C. (Matthiae in Orthmann 1975, 467-73). And certainly one of the most significant contributions of the discovery of the Royal Palace G of Early Syrian Ebla is just in the fact that it stands out, with the spatial conception which is realized in it, as one of the monuments which is at the origin of an architectural history which has to be thought of in terms of unity, continuity and originality.

	NORTHERN MESOPOTAMIA			NORTHERN SYRIA				
3500	Early Uruk	Ninive III	Gawra XIIA-XI		Amuq F	Mardikh I	Tarsus Late Chalc.	Proto-Historical
3400	Middle Uruk							
3300	Late Uruk	Ninive IV	Gawra XA-IX		Amuq G			
3200								
3100	Jamdat Nasr		Gawra VIIIC-A	Early Bronze I		— ? ↓ — —	Tarsus EB I	Proto-Urban
3000								
2900	Early Dynastic I	Ninive V	Gawra VII	Early Bronze II		— ? ↑ — —	Tarsus EB II	Early Syrian IA
2800						Mardikh IIA		
2700	Early Dynastic II			Early Bronze III	Amuq H			Early Syrian IB
2600	Early Dynastic IIIa							Early Syrian IC
2500	Early Dynastic IIIb							
2400								
2300	Akkad	Assur G	Gawra VI	Early Bronze IVA	Amuq I	Mardikh IIB1	Tarsus EB IIIa	Early Syrian IIA
2200	Post-Akkad Lagash II	Assur F		Early Bronze IVB	Amuq J	Mardikh IIB2	Tarsus EB IIIb	Early Syrian IIB
2100	Ur III	Assur E	Gawra V					
2000								

Catalog of Ceramic Forms

Profiles shown in Figure 3

FIELD NUMBER	TYPE	SQUARE	LOCUS	LEVEL	DESCRIPTION
1 – TM.75.G.510/3	Goblet	DiV5i+DIV5iv*	L. 2812	5	Wheel-made; white yellow clay; small and medium black and white grit; very fine ware; corrugated surface.
2 – TM.75.G.215/4	Cup	DiV7i+DiV7iv	L. 2718	Floor	Wheel-made; pink-brown clay; small black and white grit; very fine ware.
3 – TM.75.G.510/1	Goblet	DiV5i+DIV5iv	L. 2812	5	Wheel-made; brown-white clay; small black grit; very fine ware.
4 – TM.75.G.216/30	Goblet	DiV7i+DiV7iv	L. 2718	Floor	Wheel-made; brown-white clay; small black grit; very fine ware; corrugated surface.
5 – TM.75.G.189/5	Goblet	DIV6ii	L. 2712	Floor	Wheel-made; green clay; small black grit; very fine ware.
6 – TM.75.G.520/2	Goblet	DiV5i+DIV5iv	L. 2812	5	Wheel-made; white clay; small black grit; very fine ware.
7 – TM.75.G.216/26	Goblet	DiV7i+DiV7iv	L. 2718	Floor	Wheel-made; pink-brown clay; small black and white grit; very fine ware; white burnished corrugated surface.
8 – TM.75.G.216/20	Goblet	DiV7i+DiV7iv	L. 2718	Floor	Wheel-made; white clay; small and medium black and white grit; very fine ware; corrugated surface.
9 – TM.75.G.216/21	Goblet	DiV7i+DiV7iv	L. 2718	Floor	Wheel-made; brown-white clay; small and medium black and white grit; very fine ware; corrugated surface.
10 – TM.75.G.216/33	Goblet	DiV7I+DiV7iv	L. 2718	Floor	Wheel-made; red and white clay; small black and white grit; very fine ware; corrugated surface.
11 – TM.75.G.216/23	Goblet	DiV7i+DiV7iv	L. 2718	Floor	Wheel-made; white-grey clay; small black grit; very fine ware; corrugated surface.
12 – TM.75.G.510/12	Cup	DiV5i+DIV5iv	L. 2812	5	Wheel-made; brown-green clay; small black grit; vegetable inclusions; very fine ware.
13 – TM.75.G.510/24	Cup	DiV5I+DIV5iv	L. 2812	5	Hand-made; clay red inside white outside; small black, white and brown grit; very fine ware.
14 – TM.75.G.510/11	Cup	DiV5i+DIV5iv	L. 2812	5	Wheel-made; pink-brown clay; small black grit; very fine ware.

*Squares marked as Di and DI are adjacent to each other as Italian does not contain the letters j or k. [Editor's note.]

Profiles shown in Figure 4

FIELD NUMBER	TYPE	SQUARE	LOCUS	LEVEL	DESCRIPTION
1 – TM.75.G.189/4	Juglet	DIV6ii	L. 2712	Floor	Wheel-made; white-green clay; small black and brown grit; fine ware; black paint.
2 – TM.75.G.189/1	Juglet	DIV6ii	L. 2712	Floor	Wheel-made; brown-grey clay; small black grit; fine ware; reserved slip.
3 – TM.75.G.510/35bis	Jar	DiV5i+DIV5iv	L. 2812	5	Wheel-made; pink-brown clay; small black and white grit; very fine ware.
4 – TM.75.G.510/27	Jar	DiV5i+DIV5iv	L. 2812	5	Wheel-made; whitish clay; small black and white grit; fine ware; black paint.
5 – TM.75.G.160/13	Jar				Hand-made; brown-grey core, pink-brown clay; small black and white grit; vegetable inclusions; medium fine ware.
6 – TM.75.G.510/38	Jar	DiV5i+DIV5iv	L. 2812	4+5	Hand-made; brown-grey clay; small white and grey grit; fine ware.
7 – TM.75.G.510/35	Jar	DiV5i+DIV5iv	L. 2812	4+5	Hand-made; wheel-made rim; brown-grey core; pink-brown clay; small black and white grit; fine ware.

List of Figures

List of Plates

Ill. 5. Tell Mardikh – Ebla,
the "Ceremonial Staircase" from the West

Ill. 6. Tell Mardikh – Ebla,
the door to the "Ceremonial Staircase" from the East.

Ill. 7. Tell Mardikh – Ebla, the South ramp of the "Ceremonial Staircase" from the West.

Ill. 8. Tell Mardikh – Ebla, the North ramp of the "Ceremonial Staircase" from the East.

Ill. 9. Tell Mardikh – Ebla, the portal on the East façade from the West.

Ill. 10. Tell Mardikh – Ebla, L.2764 from the South-West.

Ill. 11. Tell Mardikh – Ebla, the stairway of Mardikh IIB2 from the South.

Ill. 12. Tell Mardikh – Ebla, the storeroom L.2712 from the South.

Ill. 13. Tell Mardikh – Ebla, the library L.2769 from the West.

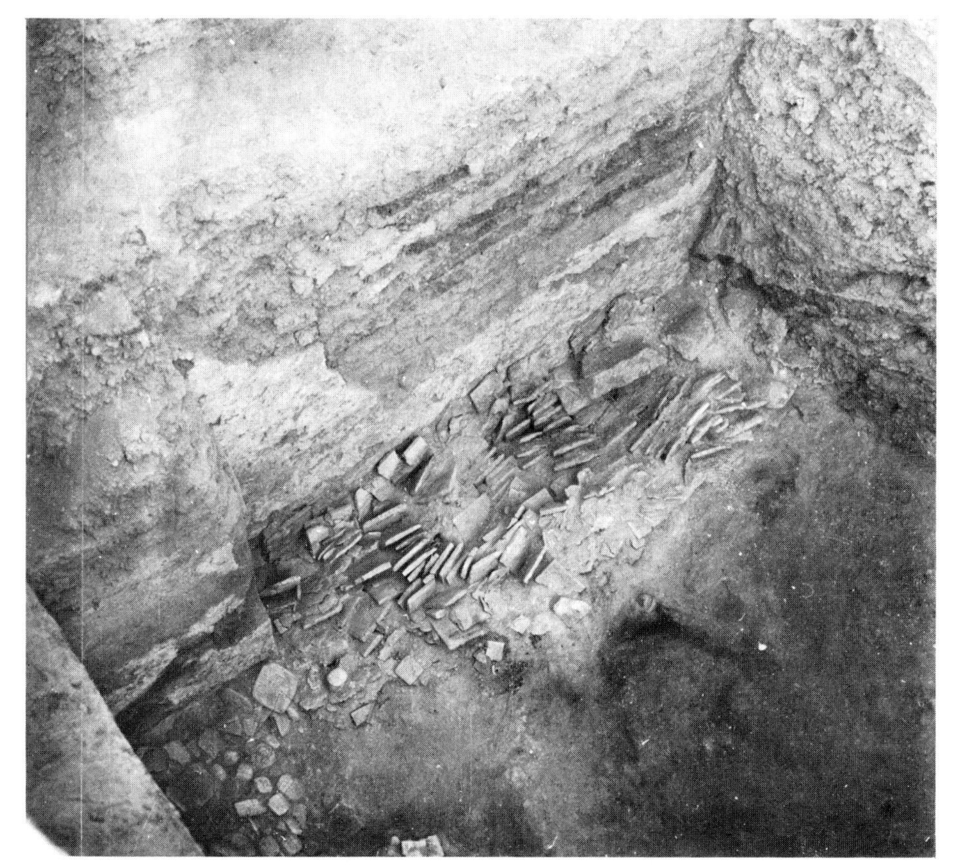

Ill. 14. Tell Mardikh – Ebla, the eastern wall of the library L.2769 from the North-West.

Ill. 15. Tell Mardikh – Ebla, the cuneiform tablets against the Northern wall from the South.

Ill. 16. Tell Mardikh – Ebla,
a wooden carving with a lion attacking a goat from L.2601.

Ill. 17. Tell Mardikh – Ebla,
feminine figure, wooden carving from L.2601.

11. Tell Mardikh – Ebla, the stairway of Mardikh IIB2 from South.
12. Tell Mardikh – Ebla, the storeroom L.2712 from South.
13. Tell Mardikh – Ebla, the library L.2769 from West.
14. Tell Mardikh – Ebla, the eastern wall of the library L.2769 from North-West.
15. Tell Mardikh – Ebla, the cuneiform tablets against the Northern wall from South.
16. Tell Mardikh – Ebla, a wooden carving with a lion attacking a goat from L.2601.
17. Tell Mardikh – Ebla, feminine figure, wooden carving from L.2601.

References

BAHNASSI, A. (Ed.)
1974 *Antiquités de l'Euphrate. Exposition des découvertes de la Campagne Internationale de sauvegarde des antiquités de l'Euphrate* (Alep).

BRAIDWOOD, R. J. and L. S.
1969 *Excavations in the Plain of Antioch, I. The Earlier Assemblages. Phases A-J.* Oriental Institute Publications LXI (Chicago).

DELOUGAZ, P. and S. LLOYD
1942 *Pre-Sargonid Temples in the Diyala Region.* Oriental Institute Publications LVIII (Chicago).

DOLCE, R.
1975 Su alcuni resti di intarsi protodinastici da Tell Mardikh, *Oriens Antiquus,* XIV, 289-306.

EHRICH, R. W. (Ed.)
1965 *Chronologies in Old World Archaeology* (Chicago-London).

FRANKFORT, H.
1954 *The Art and Architecture of the Ancient Orient* (Harmondsworth).

FUGMANN, E.
1958 *Hama. Fouilles et recherches de la Fondation Carlsberg 1931-1938, II 1. L'architecture des périodes pré-hellénistiques* (København).

GADD, C. J.
1966 *The Dynasty of Agade and the Gutian Invasion.* The Cambridge Ancient History, Vol. I, Chapter XIX (Cambridge).

GELB, I. J.
1977 Thoughts about Ibla: A Preliminary Evaluation, March 1977, *Syro-Mesopotamian Studies,* 1/1, 3-30.

HIRSCH, H.
1963 Die Inschriften der Könige von Agade, *Archiv für Orientforschung,* XX, 1-82.

LENZEN, H. J.
1968 *XXIV. vorläufiger Bericht über die von dem Deutschen Archäologischen Institut und der Deutschen Orient-Gesellschaft aus Mitteln der Deutschen Forschungsgemeinschaft unternommenen Ausgrabungen in Uruk-Warka. Winter 1965/66* (Berlin).

MALLOWAN, M. E. L.
1947 Excavations at Brak and Chagar Bazar, *Iraq,* IX, 1-259.

MARGUERON, J. C.
1974 Les palais de l'Age du Bronze en Mésopotamie, P. Garelli (ed.), *Le Palais et la Royauté. XIXe Rencontre Assyriologique Internationale,* 11-26 (Paris).

MATTHIAE, P.
1974 A Fragment of a "Second Transition Period" Statuette from Tell Mardikh, *Baghdader Mitteilungen,* VII, 125-37.
1975 Ebla nel periodo delle dinastie amorree e della dinastia di Akkad. Scoperte archeologiche recenti a Tell Mardikh, *Orientalia,* XLIV, 337-60.

MATTHIAE, P.

1976a Ebla à l'époque d'Akkad: archéologie et histoire, *Comptes Rendus de l'Académie des Inscriptions et Belles-Lettres*, Octobre, 190-215.

1976b Ibla. B. Archäologisch, *Reallexikon der Assyriologie und vorderasiatischen Archäologie*, Vol. V, 13-20 (Berlin-New York).

1976c La scoperta del Palazzo Reale G e degli Archivi di Stato di Ebla (ca. 2400-2250 a.C.), *La Parola del Passato*, XXXI, 233-66.

1976d La biblioteca reale di Ebla (2400-2250 a.C.): risultati della Missione Archeologica Italiana in Siria, 1975, *Rendiconti della Pontificia Accademia Romana di Archeologia, 1975-1976*, XLVIII, 19-45.

1977 Tell Mardikh: The Archives and Palace, *Archaeology* 30, 244-53.

MATTHIAE, P. and G. PETTINATO

1976 Aspetti amministrativi e topografici di Ebla nel III millennio av. Cr. A. Documentazione epigrafica, B. Considerazioni archeologiche, *Rivista degli Studi Orientali*, L, 1-30.

MOOREY, P. R. S.

1964 The "Plano-Convex Building" at Kish and Early Mesopotamian Palaces, *Iraq*, XXVI, 83-98.

MOORTGAT, A.

1967 *Die Kunst des Alten Mesopotamian* (Köln).

1968 Frühe Kanaanäisch-Sumerische Berührungen in Mari, *Baghdader Mitteilungen*, IV, 221-31.

ORTHMANN, W. (Ed.)

1975 *Propyläen Kunstgeschichte, XIV. Der Alte Orient* (Berlin).

PARROT, A.

1972 Les fouilles de Mari. Vingtième campagne de fouilles (Printemps 1972), *Syria*, XLIX, 281-302.

PETTINATO, G.

1975 Testi cuneiformi del 3. millennio in paleocananeo rinvenuti nella campagna 1974 a Tell Mardikh-Ebla, *Orientalia*, XLIV, 361-74.

1976a The Royal Archives of Tell Mardikh-Ebla, *Biblical Archeologist*, XXXIX, 44-52.

1976b Ibla. A. Philologisch, *Reallexikon der Assyriologie und vorderasiatische Archäologie*, Vol. V, 9-13 (Berlin-New York).

SOLLBERGER, E. and J.-R. KUPPER

1971 *Inscriptions Royales Sumériennes et Akkadiennes.*

TADMOR, M.

1964 Contacts Between the ʿAmuq and Syria-Palestine, *IEJ*, XIV, 253-69.

WOOLLEY, C. L.

1955 *Alalakh. An Account of the Excavations at Tell Atchana in the Hatay, 1937-1949* (Oxford).

1974 *Ur Excavations, VI. The Buildings of the Third Dynasty* (London-Philadelphia).

Additional Note (February 1978)

The development of the excavations in the area of the Royal Palace G of Mardikh IIB1 aimed in 1976 at the definition of the "Audience Court" and in 1977 at the delimitation of the Administrative Quarter. The exploration of 1976 has allowed us to establish that, most probably, the Court had a length, along the North-South axis, of nearly m. 52.00, while the soundings made along the line of the North façade of the Court have shown that all remains of the Mardikh IIB1 settlement have disappeared beyond the already identified point of interruption of the structures of the Court. We could establish that the sector of the Administrative Quarter built outside the Palace G, that is under the East porch of the Court, consisted of at least two rooms, the archive L.2769, which, on the basis of the 1976 excavations is 5.10 by 3.55 in size, and the antechamber L.2875. The excavations made in 1977 in the area of the Administrative Quarter inside the East façade of the Court, that is the real area of Palace G, made us identify three rooms which form an autonomous complex with respect to the rest of the Palace. They are L.2764 to the North, where a staircase has been built which went to the second floor surely existent everywhere in the area of the Administrative Quarter; L.2913 in the middle, possibly a small court with a porch with four columns, on which opened the gate from the Court to the Administrative Quarter; it is possible that this court had a loggia on the second floor, decorated by important artifacts of which we have found some remarkable fragments; L.2866 to the South, a wide room, the roof of which was supported by two columns, which made of it the largest room of the complex, surely used as a reception room.

DOLCE, R.
1977 Nuovi frammenti di intarsi da Tell Mardikh-Ebla, *Oriens Antiquus,* XVI, 1-24.
FRONZAROLI, P.
1977 West Semitic Toponymy in Northern Syria in the Third Millennium B.C., *Journal of Semitic Studies,* XXII, 145-66.
MATTHIAE, P.
1976e Ebla. Fouilles de Tell Mardikh, *Encyclopaedia Universalis, Universalia 1975*, Paris, 193-96.
1976f Ebla in the Late Early Syrian Period: the Royal Palace and the State Archives, *Biblical Archeologist,* XXXIX, 94-113.
1977b Le Palais Royal et les Archives d'Etat d'Ebla protosyrienne, *Akkadica,* 2, 2-19.
1977c Le palais Royal protosyrien d'Ebla: nouvelles recherches archéologiques à Tell Mardikh en 1976, *Comptes Rendus de l'Académie des Inscriptions et Belles-Lettres,* Avril, 148-72.
1977d *Ebla. Un impero ritrovato* (Torino).
PETTINATO, G.
1976c I testi cuneiformi della biblioteca reale di Tell Mardikh-Ebla. Notizia preliminare sulla scuola di Ebla, *Rendiconti della Pontificia Accademia Romana di Archeologia, 1975-1976,* XLVIII, 47-57.
1977a Il calendario di Ebla al tempo del re Ibbi-Sipish sulla base di TM.75.G.427, *Archiv für Orientforschung,* XXV, 1-36.
1977b Relations entre les royaumes d'Ebla et de Mari au troisième millénaire d'après les archives royales de Tell Mardikh-Ebla, *Akkadica,* II, 20-28.
1977c Gli archivi reali di Tell Mardikh-Ebla. Riflessioni e prospettive, *Rivista Biblica Italiana,* XXV, 225-43.

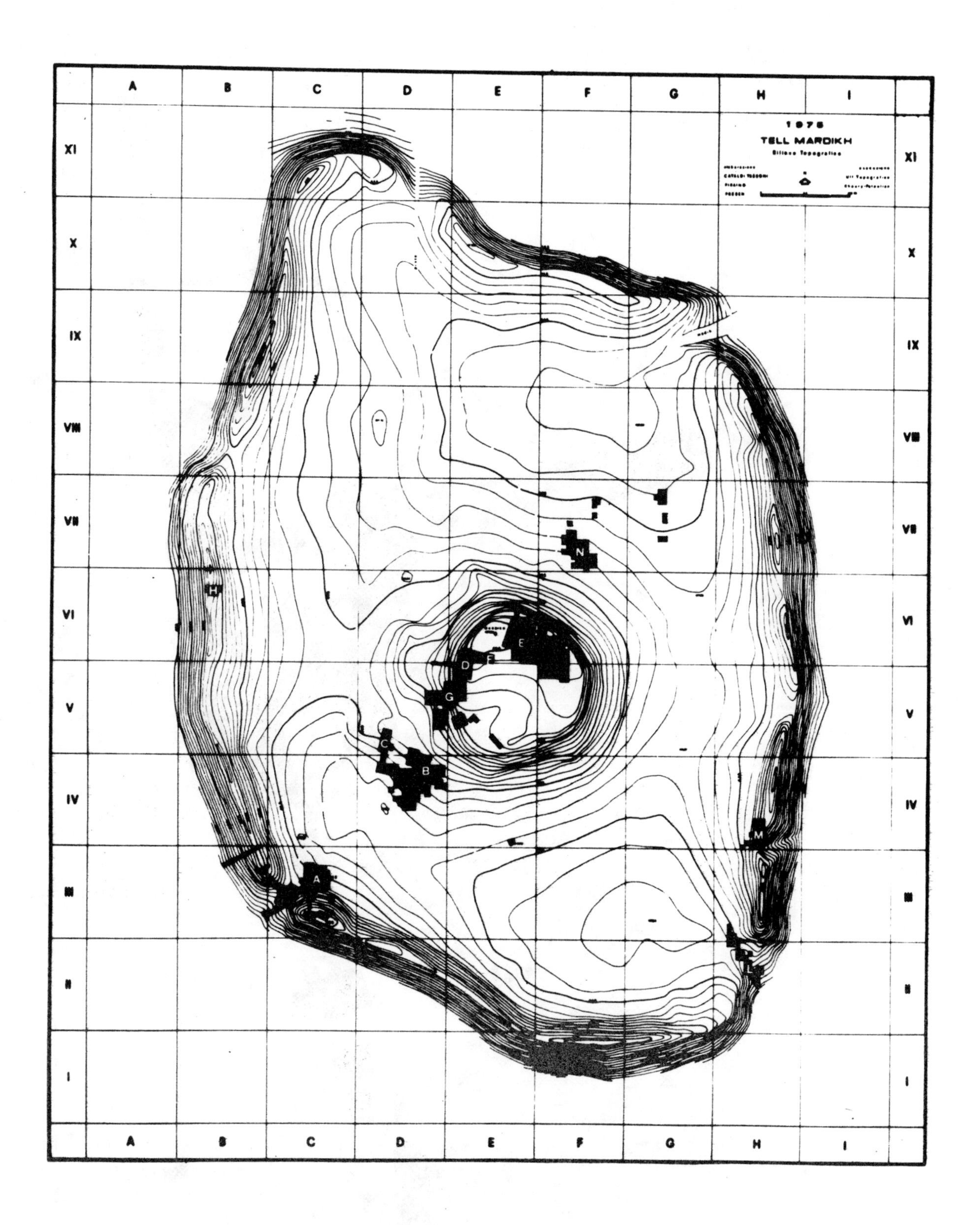

Figure 1. Tell Mardikh – Ebla, topographic plan of the tell.

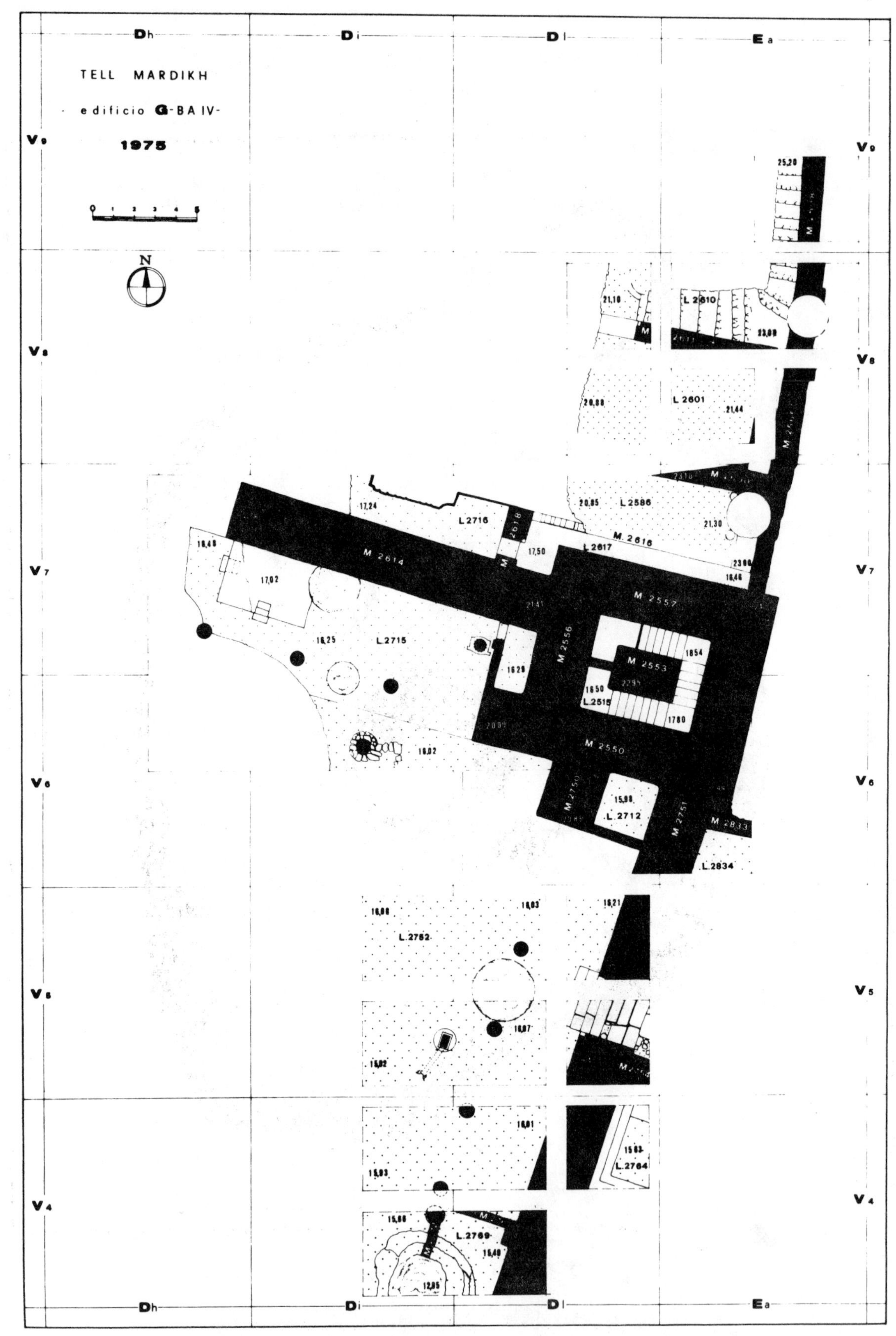

Figure 2. Tell Mardikh – Ebla, summary plan of the remains of the Royal Palace G.

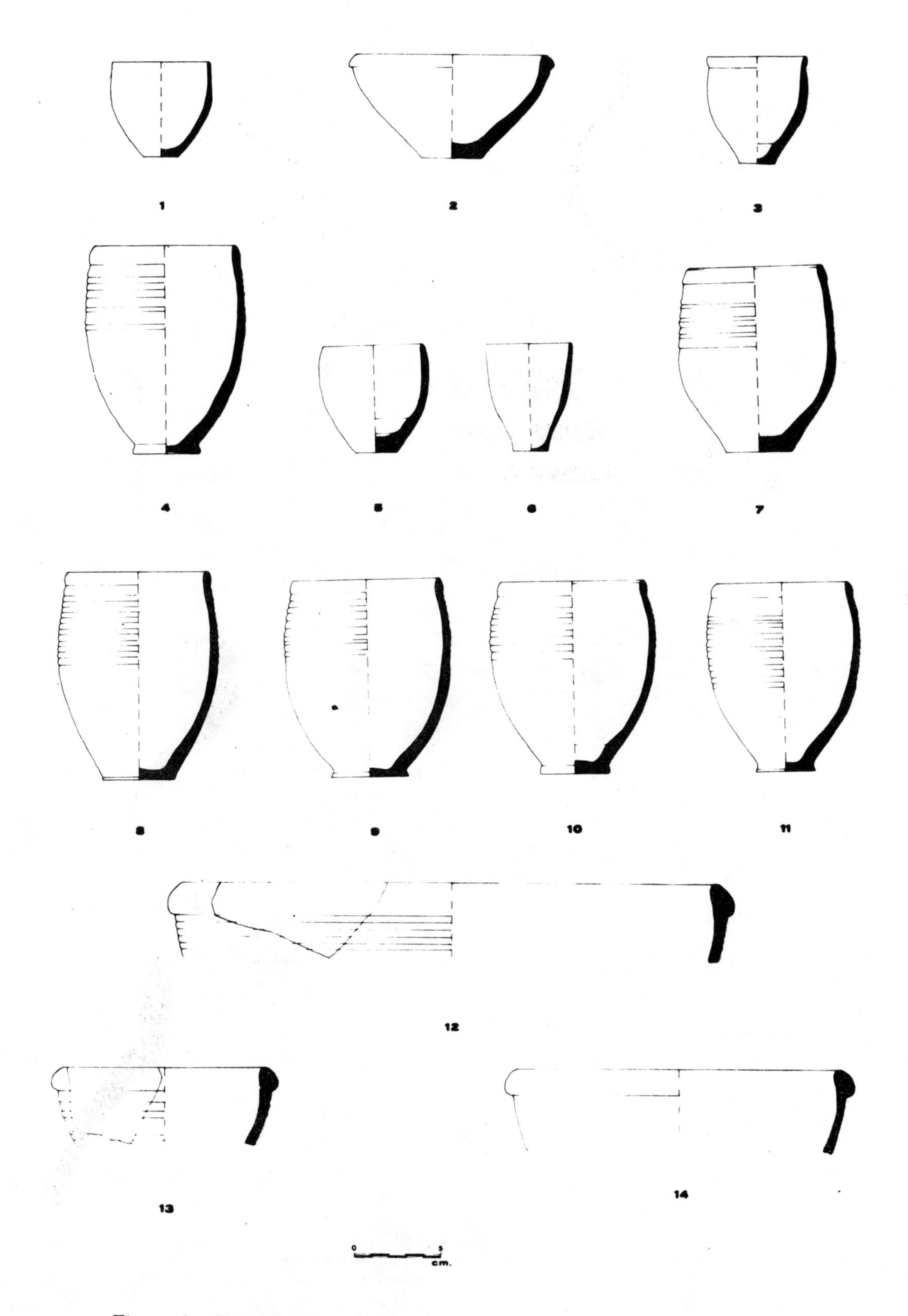

Figure 3. Tell Mardikh – Ebla, pottery of Mardikh IIB1 (Royal Palace G).

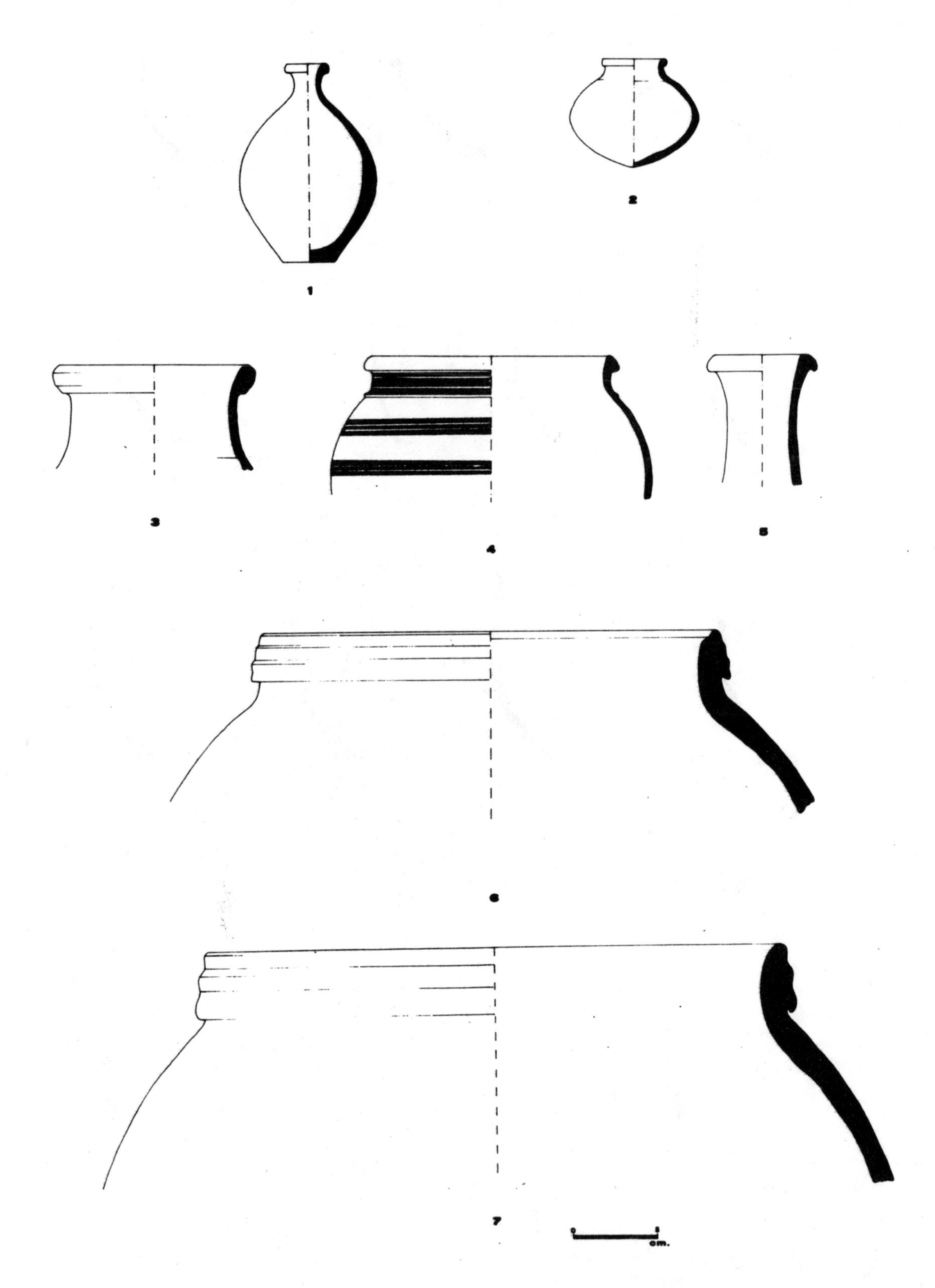

Figure 4. Tell Mardikh – Ebla, pottery of Mardikh IIB1 (Royal Palace G).

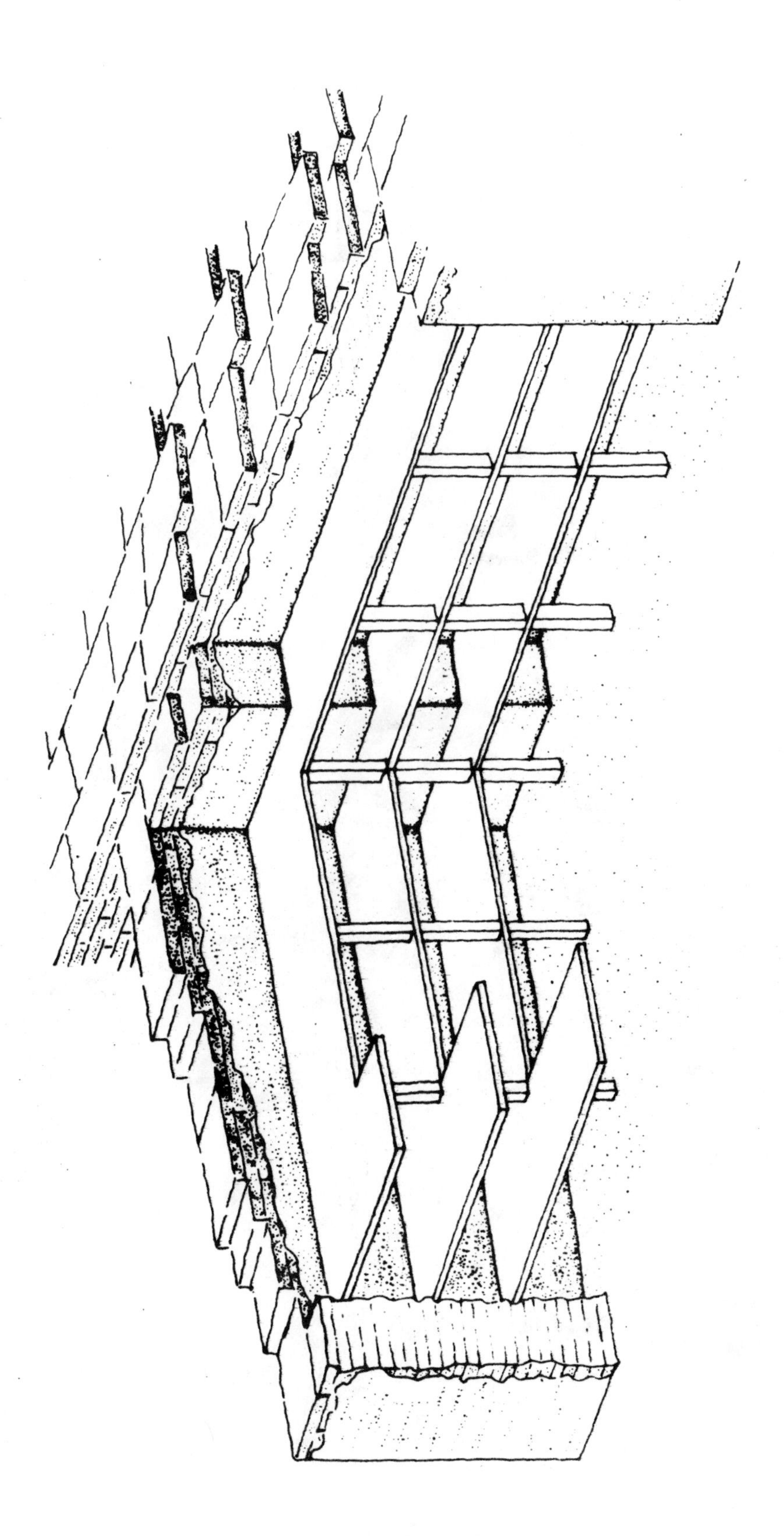

Figure 5. Tell Mardikh – Ebla, library L.2769, reconstruction of the shelves.

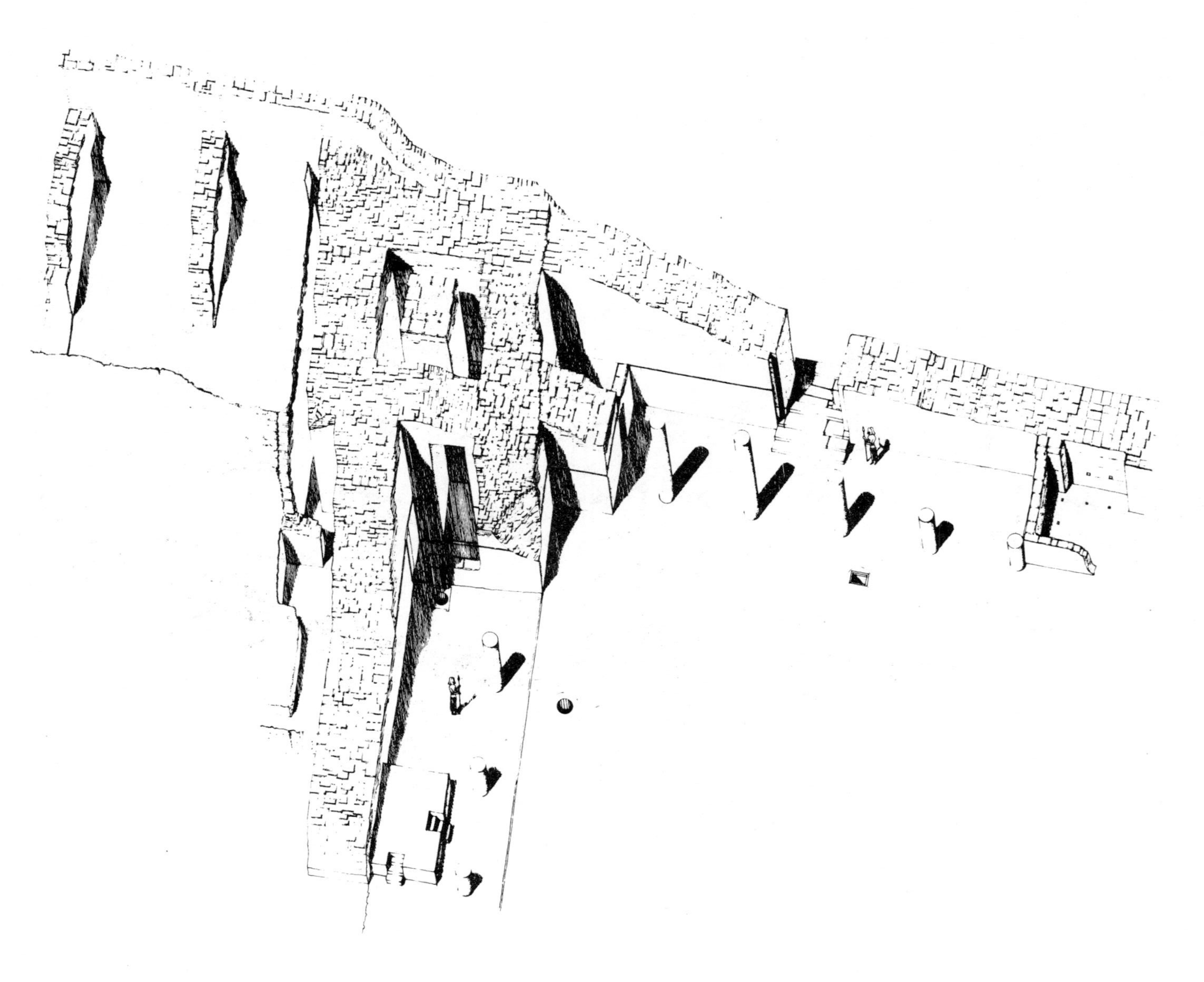

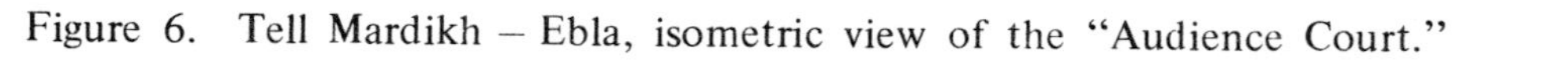

Figure 6. Tell Mardikh – Ebla, isometric view of the "Audience Court."

COMMUNIQUÉ
OF THE ITALIAN ARCHAEOLOGICAL MISSION TO SYRIA
CONCERNING THE FIRST MEETING
OF THE INTERNATIONAL COMMITTEE FOR THE STUDY OF THE TEXTS OF EBLA

The International Committee for the study of Ebla texts of the Italian Archaeological Mission to Syria of the University of Rome, composed of Messrs. G. Buccellati (Los Angeles), D. O. Edzard (München), P. Fronzaroli (Firenze), P. Garelli (Paris), H. Klengel (Berlin), J.-R. Kupper (Liège), G. Pettinato (Roma), F. Rashid (Baghdad), E. Sollberger (London), under the chairmanship of Mr. P. Matthiae, has held its first meeting in Rome, from January 11th to 14th and in Damascus from January 15th to 19th, 1978.

The Committee has prepared a plan of work and collaboration for the edition of the cuneiform texts of the Archives of the Royal Palace of Tell Mardikh-Ebla and for the establishment of secondary studies based on the readings of these texts.

The texts will be published in a collection of volumes with the title "Archivi Reali di Ebla, Testi" (ARET); the secondary studies will appear in the series "Archivi Reali di Ebla, Studi" (ARES). The two series, published by the University of Rome, will appear under the direction of Mr. Matthiae; the editorial board will be composed of the members of the International Committee for the study of Ebla texts. A journal called "Annali di Ebla" will be published by the University of Rome under the direction of Mr. Matthiae.

As regards the edition, upon a proposal of the Committee, Mr. Matthiae has given to the following authors the task of publishing the first volumes:

ARET I. Testi amministrativi della sala L. 2586 (G. Pettinato);
ARET II. Testi amministrativi dell'archivio L. 2712, 1 (G. Pettinato);
ARET III. Testi amministrativi dell'archivio L. 2769, 1. Tessili (A. Archi);
ARET IV. Testi amministrativi dell'archivio L. 2769, 2. Varii (D. O. Edzard);
ARET V. Testi amministrativi dell'archivio L. 2769, 3. Tessili (L. Cagni);
ARET VI. Testi amministrativi dell'archivio L. 2712, 2 (G. Pettinato);
ARET VII. Testi amministrativi dell'archivio L. 2769, 4. Tessili (C. Zaccagnini);
ARET VIII. Testi amministrativi dell'archivio L. 2769, 5. Tessili (E. Sollberger);
ARET IX. Testi amministrativi dell'archivio L. 2712, 3 (G. Pettinato);
ARET X. Testi amministrativi dell'archivio L. 2769, 6. Metalli (A. Archi).

In order to prepare the preliminary materials which will allow the elaboration of a plan of edition of other categories of texts Mr. Pettinato will prepare a report about the lexical texts; Mr. Fronzaroli and Mr. Pettinato about the lexical texts with Eblaite glosses; Mr. Edzard, Mr. Fronzaroli, Mr. Kupper and Mr. Pettinato about the documents of historical character; Mr. Rashid about administrative texts concerning textiles, in view of the preparation of volume XI.

As regards the secondary studies in the sphere of the principal fields of research, the work to establish the syllabary will be undertaken by Mr. Buccellati, Mr. Edzard, Mr. Fronzaroli, Mr. Pettinato and Mr. Sollberger; Mr. Fonzaroli has been charged with the study of the phonology and in general of the linguistic aspects of Eblaite; Mr. Buccellati will study the Semitic personal names; Mr. Garelli and

Mr. Kupper, with the collaboration of Mr. Matthiae, will undertake the study of the toponymy and the historic topography. Mr. H. Klengel and Mr. M. Liverani will be in charge of studies of a historical character related mostly to social and economic aspects.